Sparks of Truth

Sidelights on

Demonstration

EMMET FOX

Martino Publishing
Mansfield Centre, CT
2011

Martino Publishing
P.O. Box 373,
Mansfield Centre, CT 06250 USA

www.martinopublishing.com

ISBN   978-1-61427-061-4

© 2011   Martino Publishing

Cover design by T. Matarazzo

Printed in the United States of America On 100% Acid-Free Paper

Sparks of Truth

Sidelights on
Demonstration

EMMET FOX

CHURCH OF THE HEALING CHRIST
Astor Hotel - New York

25 Cents

I.N.T·A., Ltd.
1, Henrietta Place, London, W.1.

CONTENTS

CONTENTS—(*continued*)

These Sparks originally appeared
as weekly messages on the
Sunday Programs.

*A small spark can start a
great fire.*

TAKE IT EASY

DON'T HURRY. You are going to live forever—somewhere. In fact, you are in eternity now; so why rush?

Don't Worry. What will this thing matter in twenty years' time? You belong to God, and God is Love; so why fret?

Don't Condemn. As you cannot get under the other fellow's skin, you cannot possibly know what difficulties he has had to meet—how much temptation, or misunderstanding, or stupidity within himself he has had to overcome. You are not perfect yourself and might be much worse in his shoes. Judge not!

Don't Resent. If wrong has been done, the Great Law will surely take care of it. Rise up in consciousness and set both yourself and the delinquent free. Forgiveness is the strongest medicine.

Don't Grumble. Consume your own smoke. Your own concept is what you see; so treat, and change that.

Don't Grab. You cannot hold what does not belong to you by right of consciousness anyway. Grabbing postpones your good.

Don't Shove. You are always in your right place at the moment. If you don't like it, change it scientifically by rising in consciousness. This will be permanent.

AN ALL IN POLICY

WHAT has your religion done for you? For years probably, you have been attending church, reading spiritual books, studying the Bible, and so forth. Now I suggest that you have a spiritual stock-taking. Ask yourself—what has your religion done for you? What difference has it made in your life, in your home, in your affairs? How much peace of mind has it given you? How much courage? How much understanding? How much opportunity for service? For, make no mistake, real religion does give all these things.

If your spiritual stock-taking does not turn out to be satisfactory, if your religion is not working in this way—if on examining your life you find there are a number of places at which you are not demonstrating, if certain needs are still lacking to you, if there are still negative things that refuse to go—I believe that you will find the explanation to lie in the following law: *What you put into your religion, that you get out of it.*

If you put five per cent of yourself and your life into your religion, you will receive a five per cent dividend or demonstration. If you put twenty per cent of yourself and your life into your religion, you will receive a twenty per cent demonstration. And until you put one hundred per cent of yourself and your life into your religion you will not receive a one hundred per cent demonstration.

A complete, all round demonstration calls for an *all in* policy.

SALUTING THE CHRIST IN HIM

WE OFTEN hear the expression "saluting the Christ in him," or "seeing the Christ in him," and we may well ask ourselves what that phrase really means. Well, it is simply the practical application of the rule of Jesus Christ, "Judge not according to appearances but judge righteous judgment."

Each one of us has a Divine Self which is spiritual and perfect but which is never seen on this plane. That is the true man, God's man, and is what we call today, "the Christ within." It is the *real* you, or the *real* he, or she.

Now whenever you dwell upon or realize the presence of the Christ within—within yourself or within anyone else—outer appearances begin at once to improve, and both the amount of the improvement and the rate at which it takes place, will depend on the number of times that the Indwelling

11

Christ is "saluted" or realized, and the degree of realization attained.

This saluting of the Christ need take only a moment, and it never fails to benefit the individual concerned, and the person who does it also.

When someone seems to be behaving badly, or when you hear bad news concerning him, salute the Christ in him instead of accepting the appearance. When a given condition seems to be inharmonious, whether it be an organ of the body, a business arrangement, or anything else, see God working in it—better still, *"Golden Key"* it—and this saluting of the Christ will heal it.

If somebody displeases you, silently salute the Christ in him, and say aloud whatever seems best. If someone says: "John Smith is sick," salute the Christ in Smith (know that in reality he is spiritual and perfect), and refuse to accept the negative statement. If someone says something against John Smith's character, salute the Christ in him, refuse to discuss the matter, and of course do not repeat it.

12

The oftener you salute the Christ in others, the sooner will you find It in yourself.

BLESSING AND CURSING

LIFE is a reflex of mental states. As far as *you* are concerned, the character that things will bear will be the character that you first impress upon them. *Bless a thing and it will bless you. Curse it and it will curse you.* If you put your condemnation upon anything in life, it will hit back at you and hurt you. If you bless any situation, it has no power to hurt you, and even if it is troublesome for a time it will gradually fade out—if you sincerely bless it.

We are told, you remember, that whatever name Adam gave to an animal—that was its name; and of course you know that the name of a thing means its character. Adam said to one animal, "You are a tiger, ferocious," and so it was. To another, he said, "You are a gazelle, gentle and kind," and so it was. Now, Adam is Everyman, and until we learn to give good names, to "christen" everything, we shall have enemies of various kinds to deal with.

14

Bless your body. If there is anything wrong with a particular organ, bless that organ. (Of course, you must bless the organ and not the disease.) Bless your home. Bless your business. Bless your associates. Turn any seeming enemies into friends by blessing them. Bless the climate. Bless the town, and the state, and the country.

Bless a thing and it will bless you.

STAND BY FOR QUARANTINE!

WHEN you are praying or treating about a particular thing, you should handle it, mentally, very carefully indeed. The ideal way is not to think about it at all except when you are actually praying about it. To think about it in between, especially to talk to other people about it, is exceedingly likely to invite failure.

When a new problem presents itself to you, you should immediately know the Truth about it, and then decline to consider it except in the light of Truth. I call this "putting a subject in quarantine," and whenever I have been able to "quarantine" a problem of my own I have always demonstrated very easily and very well.

Even an old, long-standing problem can be "put in quarantine" today, if you mean business and will resolutely break the habit of constantly thinking over that problem.

Everyone knows that a photographer

16

must not expose unfixed film to daylight, if he wants to get results. Everyone knows how careful a chemist is to isolate (i.e., "quarantine") his materials in the laboratory, since the slightest contamination of one chemical by another will probably ruin any experiment. What many Truth students do not seem to understand is that mental operations have to be just as carefully safeguarded if demonstrations are to be made.

Whenever you think about any subject, you are treating it with your thought—either for good or evil.

THE WILL OF GOD

THE most wonderful thing in the world is the Will of God. The Will of God for you at the present moment is something glorious and beautiful, thrillingly interesting and joyous, and, in fact, far beyond anything that you could possibly sit down and wish for with your conscious mind.

It is unfortunate that so many people seem to assume as a matter of course that the Will of God for them is likely to be something dull or burdensome, if not positively repulsive.

"I suppose it is God's will for me, so I must put up with it," people say when talking about some condition that they hate. "Thy will be done," pious people say in the face of death or tragedy. All this is absolutely wrong. The Will of God for man is life, health, happiness, and true self-expression, and it is only in connection with these things that we can say, "Thy will be done."

18

Trouble or suffering of any kind does not come from God. It is an indication that there is a lesson to be learned by us, and the trouble itself furnishes us with the very opportunity that we need in order to learn that lesson, so that such a thing need never happen to us again.

Trouble is valuable opportunity. Experience is priceless instruction. The Will of God for you is always something joyous and fine.

SPREADING THE TRUTH*

TO CONVEY the knowledge of the Truth to others has always been considered one of the most effective means for one's own spiritual development. In the ancient schools of Wisdom it was an accepted duty regarded as binding upon all. Jesus himself has said to us: "Go ye therefore and teach all nations," and, "This gospel must first be preached to all the world."

In this age when practically everyone can read and write, the circulation of inexpensive booklets and pamphlets, is one of the most effective ways of spreading the Truth. A written statement is impersonal. It raises no arguments. It is never inopportune, because the recipient will naturally wait until he is ready before reading it. It can be gone over several times at leisure if it is not readily understood at first contact.

You cannot do a more useful thing for

* See *Fifteen Points* card, No. 7.

your fellow man, and for yourself too, than
to put in somebody else's way any one
of the Truth books that have helped you
personally. This practice, in Shakespeare's
phrase, "is twice blessed. It blesseth him
that gives and him that takes."

Hear a modern parable:

John Smith bought a Truth book. He
handed it or mailed it to his friend, Mr.
Brown, whom he knew to be going through
a difficult time. Brown was immensely struck
with it—these ideas were quite new to him
—he carried the little book about in his
pocket, followed the instruction given, and
made a beautiful demonstration. He was
so enthusiastic that he broached the subject to a business colleague, Jones, during
lunch, presented him with his own copy,
and wrote off for a fresh supply for himself
that night.

Jones, as it happened, was not really in-
terested. He took the little book merely
out of politeness, glanced at the first page,
and threw it away. He was about to tear
it across as was his custom when discarding

documents, but the attractive cover restrain-
ed him and he put it aside uninjured.

His stenographer, Miss Robinson, found
it among the litter, and, liking the look of
it, took it home and studied it carefully.
She determined to try it on a personal
problem that was making her own life mis-
erable at the time, and being unusually
simple and direct in her methods, demonstrated within three days. She then mailed
her copy to her brother in a distant city.
For years he had been hungry for a living
religion, and, briefly, the booklet changed
his life. Naturally he himself went on to
spread the Truth in his own way, as did each
of the others in the chain.

In this parable, we see that John Smith,
by a single act, became the means of blessing quite a number of people (most of
whom he never heard of), and that the good
results of that first act went on indefinitely.

Until the people learn the Truth, it cannot
set them free.

THE DOVE

IN PRAYER or treatment it is the thought, and not the words used, that matters. The words are merely an indication of the thought. Some people find that the right idea develops more easily when a good many words are used, and of course such people should use as many words as they feel the need of. Others are embarrassed by the difficulty of finding many words, and in that case two or three phrases only are quite sufficient. A well known man was healed of consumption using only the single statement "God is Love." Of course, he dwelt upon it intelligently until he thoroughly realized something of what those words must mean.

We all remember the story of Ali Baba and the cave. Unless one knew the exact word it was impossible to open the door. The thought might be the precise one required, but unless the exact word "sesame" was uttered, the door remained obstinately shut. Barley? Wheat? Grain?—No use.

"Sesame" was the magic word, and nothing else whatever would do. Now in treatment it is the exact opposite of this. Not the word, but the thought in mind is what counts. As long as the thought is right we may use any language that we find helpful. Our treatments are prayers and not incantations.

Often it is well to dispense with words altogether, as getting in the way, and introducing a dangerous moment of delay. When God visits His people, it is their business to welcome Him immediately, and to experience Him; not to try to form intellectual definitions. We must never keep God waiting. Directly the realization, which is Immanuel, presents itself, you may have to drop all words—cease "working" there and then, and *possess* it. If you postpone this for ever so short a time you will find, when you come to look for it, that the Dove has flown away again, and you will have to wait until he returns. And that *may* be quite a long time.

People sometimes say "I will give half

24

an hour to this case," or it may be "I will go through the Seven Main Aspects of God." Excellent things to do, but if it should happen that after three minutes, or when you have finished the second Aspect, *the Dove alights;* then receive him instantly with open arms. To think, "I will finish my treatment first," is to turn him away. This feeling of the real Presence of God is itself, of course, the perfect treatment; the end to which all our statements are but means.

He saw the heavens opened and the Spirit like a dove descending upon him (Mark 1:10).

SATAN GETS AWAY
WITH IT

GOD is the only Presence and the only Power. God is the only Cause, and His will is completely fulfilled at every moment. What we call evil or error is a false belief which we form about good. It has no power apart from the power we give it by believing in it.

This is the Truth teaching, but it happens too often in practice that the student, instead of really getting rid of the conventional belief in the reality of evil, merely changes the name of his devil, and goes on recognizing him under some new alias.

It is the standard practice with swindlers each time they are exposed, promptly to change the name of the firm and then restart the old fraud under the new style. When once the name of "John Smith" has appeared in the police reports, he does not, unless he is a very negligible villain indeed, again solicit your confidence under that title. It would be waste of time. What he does is just to buy a new brass plate and start up the old racket again as "Messrs. Brown & Jones" or what not. Later, when this in turn is exploded, he once more changes the style of the firm to, let us say, "Robinson & Company," and so on *ad infinitum*. And he never lacks victims, because so long as people will allow themselves to be swayed by mere names, instead of examining the underlying thought, they have no protection.

This is just the way in which apparent evil acts. Satan, having been thoroughly exposed as the Devil, with horns, hoofs and tail, promptly alters his name and address, and goes on tempting those who should know better, into sin, sickness, and death, by giving himself some new description such as error, mortal mind, hypnotism, time, climate, heredity, and so forth. And only too often he gets away with it quite successfully. Instead of being emancipated from fear, his victims are now ten times more under its dominion than ever they were in their orthodox days, and they suffer accordingly. They have merely changed the label on their superstition.

As long as you recognize the reality of anything but God, under any pretense, you are harboring fear, and you will punish yourself inevitably. It makes no difference whether you choose to give your bogey the name of Satan, Old Nick, Mephisto, or to call it climate, or heredity, or age, or anything else.

I am the Lord, and there is none else, there is no God beside me (Isaiah 45:5).

WHAT IS SCIENTIFIC
PRAYER?

SCIENTIFIC prayer or spiritual treatment is really the lifting of your consciousness above the level where you have met your problem. If only you can rise high enough in thought, the problem will then solve itself. That is really the only problem you have—to rise in consciousness. The more "difficult," which means the more deeply rooted in your thought, is the problem concerned, the higher you will have to rise. What is called a small trouble, will yield to a slight rise in consciousness. What is called a serious difficulty, will require a relatively higher rise. What is called a terrible danger or hopeless problem, will require a considerable rise in consciousness to overcome it—but that is the only difference.

Do not waste time trying to straighten out your own or other people's problems by manipulating thought—that gets you nowhere—but raise your consciousness, and the action of God will do the rest.

Jesus healed sick people and reformed many sinners by raising his consciousness above the picture they presented. He controlled the winds and the waves in the same way. He raised the dead because he was able to get as high in consciousness as is necessary to do this.

To raise your consciousness you must positively withdraw your attention from the picture for the time being (*The Golden Key*) and then concentrate gently upon spiritual truth. You may do this by reading the Bible or any spiritual book that appeals to you, by going over any hymn or poem that helps you in this way, or by the use of one or more affirmations, just as you like.

I know many people who have secured the necessary elevation of consciousness by browsing at random through the Bible. A man I know was saved in a terrible shipwreck by quietly reading the 91st Psalm. Another man healed himself of a supposedly hopeless disease by working on the one affirmation, "God is Love," until he was able to realize something of what that greatest of all statements must really mean.

If you work with affirmations, be careful not to get tense; but there is no reason why you should not employ all these methods in turn, and also any others that you can think of. Sometimes a talk with a spiritual person gives you just the lift that you need. It matters not how you rise so long as you do rise.

"I bore you on eagles' wings, and brought you unto Myself."

THE BIBLE UNVEILED

THE BIBLE is too often looked upon as an out-of-date and rather dull compendium of conventional religion of the sanctimonious type. There could not be, however, a greater mistake. Those who find it dull are those who have had it presented to them in the wrong way. Read in the light of the Spiritual Interpretation, it will be found to be a practical textbook of thrilling interest, containing, as it does, clear explanations and definite guidance for any and every difficulty that can arise in everyday life.

Religious difficulties, the healing of the body, the poverty problem, home or business worries, are all dealt with and provided for in the Bible.

YOU ARE A MENTAL BEING

MAN is a mental being, and to know this is the first step on the road to freedom and prosperity, for as long as you believe yourself to be primarily physical, a superior kind of animal, you will remain in bondage—in bondage, that is to say, to your own habits of thought, for there is no other bondage. Mind is primary, but mind must have embodiment, and the embodiment of your mind is found in your visible conditions—the kind of health you have, your financial position, your business connections, the sort of home you have, and all the thousand and one things that make up your present environment.

This being the case, you will see how foolish it is for you to endeavor, as do most people, to improve your conditions by altering your environment while leaving your mind unchanged. To attempt this is to attempt the impossible and to foredoom yourself to failure and disappointment. Mind is cause, and experience is effect; and so, as long as your mind remains unchanged, it will continue to produce just those effects or experiences of which you are anxious to be rid. If you do not like the experience or effect that you are getting, the obvious remedy is to alter the cause and then the effect will naturally alter too.

GOD'S HOUR

G OD'S HOUR is the most important event in the day. It may consist of thirty minutes or longer, according to the need of the individual, but it should hardly be less than that if you really mean business in your spiritual life.

God's hour is the time in which you read the Bible or other spiritual books and meditate and pray.

The practical secret of health, happiness, and prosperity, and of constant spiritual growth is to make God's hour the principal, that is to say, the most important event in your day. Let that be the center line, as it were, about which all other activities revolve. Let anything else be postponed or omitted rather than that God's hour should be neglected. Let any other engagement be cancelled in favor of this. Let any other work go undone rather than this should be missed.

God's hour need not be held at the same

time every day although it will be helpful if this can be done. The essential thing is that God's hour be the most important event in the twenty-four hours, and that everything else be secondary to that.

GOD IN BUSINESS

A LARGE proportions of what are called business problems really consist in negotiating with other people. All salesmanship, of course, is negotiation between the seller and the purchaser. And successful salesmanship means bringing that negotiation to a termination satisfactory to both parties.

Whether you be seeking a position for yourself or engaging someone else to work for you, the ultimate outcome will depend upon negotiation. You want to find the right person to fill your vacancy or you wish to be engaged for a certain position that you think would suit your requirements very well, and in either case the outcome is a matter of negotiation. Disputes and misunderstandings often arise between two business firms or between a firm and a customer, and here again harmonious relations in the future—which means more business —will depend upon how the present negotiations are conducted.

In fact, every relation in life will be found to depend upon the ability to make harmonious personal adjustments, which is negotiation. In such matters as family and personal disputes, as well as in those things more usually considered under the head of business, the same principle will be found to apply with even greater force if possible.

Now, the secret of successful negotiation can be put into a nutshell. It is this—*See God on both sides of the table*. Claim that God is working through both of you, through yourself and through the person with whom you are dealing. Do not seek by will power to get your own way, but affirm that God's will in that particular matter is being done. Remember that your own way may not be at all good for you. The very thing that you want today may turn out next week to be a nuisance or even a misfortune. Do not try to overreach the other man, to persuade him against his will, or to take the slightest advantage of him in any way. But state your case honestly to the best of your ability; do only what you think is right; and know that God is living and working in your life. Then if you do not make that sale, you will make a better one instead. If you do not get that job, you will get a better one. If you do not make the arrangement that you sought today, a better one will present itself to-morrow.

Never allow yourself to be strained or tense or over-eager. God never hurries; He works without effort. In dealing with fellow man *put God on both sides of the table*, and the outcome will be true success for both parties.

WORM GETS IDEAS

TO ME the butterfly teaches the most wonderful and the most important lesson that we human beings ever have to learn. You all know his story. He is a beautiful butterfly now, but he was not always a butterfly. No, indeed. He began life, and he lived what seemed to him a very, very long time, as a worm— and not a very important kind of worm either—what we call the humble caterpillar.

Now the life of a caterpillar is a sadly restricted one, in fact, it could be taken as the very type and symbol of restriction. He lives on a green leaf in the forest, and that is about all he knows.

Then one day something happens. The little caterpillar finds certain strange stirrings going on within himself. The old green leaf, for some reason, no longer seems sufficient. He begins to feel dissatisfied. He becomes moody and discontented, but— and this is the vital point—it is a *divine discontent*. He does not just grumble and complain to the other caterpillars, saying

40

"nature is all wrong." "I hate this life." "I can never be anything but a worm." "I wish that I had never been born." No, he is discontented, but it is a *divine discontent*. He feels the need for a bigger, finer, and more interesting life. His instinct tells him that where there is true desire there must be fulfillment, because "where there's a will, there's a way."

And so the wonderful thing happens. Gradually the worm disappears, and the butterfly emerges, beautiful, graceful, *now endowed with wings*—and instead of crawling about on a restricted leaf, he soars right above the trees, right above the forest itself —free, unrestricted, free to go where he likes, and see the world, and bask in the sun, and, in fact, be his own True Self— the free and wonderful thing that God intended him to be.

Now this wonderful story is intended to be the story of every human soul. It is up to you to develop your wings by the scientific use of creative imagination so that you may fly away to your heart's desire.

MILLENNIUM

AS the Truth of the Omnipresence and Availability of God seeps more and more into people's minds, vast changes for the better will come over the human race. These changes, in the begining at least, may be accompanied by a certain amount of confusion and apprehension, but that stage will not last very long.

First of all poverty will disappear—This change will begin in the English-speaking countries, then it will be seen in Continental Europe, and later among the other civilizations. This means the end of slums with their unholy trinity of poverty, hunger, and dirt. All will have true prosperity without victimizing one section of the community on behalf of another. Of course, this will mean the end of crime as well.

Next, sickness and disease will go. People will demonstrate healthy bodies as a matter of course and live, in full activity, to an advanced age.

So rapidly will the human consciousness improve that the thousand-and-one fears, jealousies, grudges, resentments, and so forth, that spoil people's lives today, will be absolutely a thing of the past, and war itself will cease to exist—war between nations, and industrial war too.

Think of a world with no armies and no navies, no police departments, no prisons, no hospitals, no poor houses, no orphanages, no locks on doors or drawers or banks or safe deposit vaults, because there is no need for such things.

Think of this new world, and help it to come to birth by believing it, expecting it, and praying for it.

CAUSE AND EFFECT

WHATEVER you experience in your life is really but the outpicturing of your own thoughts and beliefs. Now, you can change these thoughts and beliefs, and then the outer picture must change too. The outer picture cannot change until you change your thought. Your real heart-felt conviction is what you out-picture or demonstrate, not your mere pious opinions or formal assents.

Convictions cannot be adopted arbitrarily just because you want a healing. They are built up by the thoughts you think and the feelings you entertain day after day as you go through life. So, it is *your habitual mental conduct* that weaves the pattern of your destiny for you; and, is not this just as it should be?

So no one else can keep you out of your kingdom—or put you into it either.

The story of your life is really the story of the relations between yourself and God.

44

STUDYING THE BIBLE

FOR the spiritual study of the Bible, by far the best edition to use is the ordinary King James version. Have a Bible with type large enough to be read with comfort. A dollar or two extra spent on your Bible is worth while since you do not buy one every day.

As a general rule, it is not well to work through the Bible steadily from end to end, but rather to select any portion as you feel led at the time. Whichever section interests you most at the moment is usually likely to be best for you at that time. Read the Bible in the light of the spiritual interpretation, using the principal keys and symbols, noting the meanings of proper names, and so forth, as you come to them.

The Bible will usually give you a special message for yourself, fitting your need at the moment. In order to get this, you should claim frequently while you are reading: *"Divine Intelligence is inspiring me."*

Do not go to the Bible to get confirmation for your own ideas, but rather to be taught something new.

"Speak Lord, for Thy servant heareth."

SYMPTOMS AND CAUSES

IF you have made many efforts, as you probably have, to set things right, but without any real success, the reason is to be found just here: You have been tampering with symptoms and leaving your mind, the real cause of the trouble, untouched. You have been wrestling with circumstances, with people, and with things, and leaving your mind unchanged; and it is just that mind of yours that is causing all the trouble, all the time, and will continue to do so as long as it remains in its present state. You have been struggling to transform yourself by renewing your conditions, whereas the Law is that we are transformed by the renewing of our minds.

If you want perfect health; if you want abundant prosperity, happiness, a good home, congenial friends, beauty, joy, and thrilling interest in your life, you can have them, if you really want them; but you must want them enough to take trouble

enough to find out the only way to get
them. You must want them enough to
take the trouble to learn how to think, since
thought is the only cause.

THE CUP AND THE LIP

AN experience that comes to many people may be described as follows: In business life or in their personal affairs they frequently find themselves starting some desirable project and carrying it on without much difficulty up to the threshold of completion, whereupon, for some unknown reason it seems to jam tightly. The last step or the last two steps just cannot be taken. Seemingly everything is ready to insure success, and then at the eleventh hour, the door closes.

And this experience occurs not once but time after time in one project after another. An important sale is all but completed; all parties concerned seem to be satisfied; but when the moment for signing the contract comes, the sale falls through. Or an important position is all but secured; satisfactory interviews take place; and then at the last moment, someone else is appointed. Or an important meeting is arranged, with a great deal of pains, between

49

two people, and at the last minute the most unexpected happening prevents their meeting. And so on.

These I call "cup and lip" cases since they illustrate so well the old proverb, "There's many a slip 'twixt the cup and the lip." Such a run of misfortune can be broken in the following way: Realize: "I belong to God. My work is God's work for God works through me. God's work cannot be hindered or delayed. Of course, God always finishes successfully whatever He begins. God's work must go through to completion. My work is His work, so it reaches full fruition. I thank God for this."

HOW TO MEDITATE EASILY

T RUTH students are constantly urged
to practise meditation on Divine things
and, indeed, there is no more powerful
form of prayer. It is the Practice of the
Presence of God in its most effective form,
and is the quickest way out of sin, sickness,
and inharmony. But, unfortunately, many
people have a fixed idea that they cannot
meditate. "I am not spiritual enough,"
they say; or, "I have had no mental train-
ing along that line"; and so they cut themselves off from the quickest form of spiritual growth. Now, the fact is that everyone can and does meditate. Even the most
seemingly material people constantly meditate—only they do not meditate on Divine
things.

Thousands of men meditate deeply upon
the subject of baseball during the season,
without in the least realizing that they are
doing so. What usually happens is something like this—John Smith gets up in the
morning and immediately picks up all the

problems of life where he left them before going to sleep. He goes down to breakfast, and engages in conversation about family matters, domestic problems, and so forth. On the railroad platform he buys a paper, reads the headings on the front page, and becomes involved in national and foreign politics, and the latest crime. Then the train comes in and, having selected a seat, he turns over to the baseball page. Here he reads steadily for ten or fifteen minutes, and now a change takes place. Gradually, as he reads about the ball games and becomes absorbed in what he is reading, all other subjects fade out of his mind. Home troubles, business troubles, politics, crime, all are forgotten. Presently he lays down the paper and becomes lost in the contemplation of his subject. He thinks about prominent players. He criticises the management of his own favorite team. Possibly he thinks of certain changes which he would like to see made in the rules of the game —and much more along the same line. The next thing he knows, thirty or forty minutes have passed, and he has arrived at his destination.

Now, here is an excellent example of a first class meditation—except that it has been about baseball instead of about Divine things. This man read up his subject for ten or fifteen minutes and thus got away from the general stream of thought. Having done this, he proceeded to think through and about his subject until he became absorbed in it—his technique was perfect.

Now if you will imitate him, except that you will read a spiritual book for ten or fifteen minutes, and then think about God —taking perhaps the Seven Main Aspects in turn—think about your spiritual self, think about the Truth of Being in any shape or form, you will have made a wonderful meditation too. And if you do this you cannot fail of remarkable results.

SENTIMENT SLAYS

SENTIMENT is usually a short cut to unhappiness and failure. It is more deadly than poison gas, more cruel than the Inquisition, more subtle than self-love.

Sentiment really means pretending. It means making believe that an emotion that is really dead is still alive. It means pretending that something is fine or joyous or worth while, when in fact it is none of these things. Thus it means a waste of time, a waste of the soul substance which is lavished upon a lie. Worst of all, sentiment shuts us off from the realization of good in the present moment.

Sentiment usually pretends that some happiness is lost beyond recall, or else it persuades us to worship an unreal abstraction of some kind on the ground that actual conditions are not worth caring about.

Live in the present and let the dead past bury its dead. No good thing that ever existed is out of reach when you understand the spiritual nature of Being. See

54

to it that today and tomorrow are filled with beauty and joy, and this you can do through Treatment. Remember that people never sentimentalize over *present good;* they enjoy it, and thereby glorify God. When they sentimentalize, it is always for something supposedly out of reach.

No good experience is out of your reach because God Himself is with you.

BEAR HUGS KETTLE

I ONCE read an anecdote of the Far West which carries a wonderful metaphysical lesson. It appears that a party of hunters, being called away from their camp by a sudden alarm, left the camp fire unattended, with a kettle of water boiling on it.

Presently an old bear crept out of the woods, attracted by the fire, and, seeing the kettle with its lid dancing about on top, promptly seized it. Naturally it burnt and scalded him badly; but instead of dropping it instantly, he proceeded to hug it tightly —this being Mr. Bruin's only idea of defense. Of course, the tighter he hugged it the more it burnt him; and of course the more it burnt him the tighter he hugged it; and so on in a vicious circle, to the undoing of the bear.

This illustrates perfectly the way in which many people amplify their difficulties. They hug them to their bosoms by con-

56

stantly rehearsing them to themselves and others, and by continually dwelling upon them in every possible manner, instead of dropping them once and for all so the wound would have a chance to heal.

Whenever you catch yourself thinking about your grievances, say to yourself sternly: "Bear hugs kettle," and think about God instead. You will be surprised how quickly some long standing wounds will disappear under this treatment.

THOUGHT IS DESTINY

YOU think, and your thoughts materialize as experience; and thus it is, all unknown to yourself as a rule, that you are actually weaving the pattern of your own destiny, here and now, by the way in which you allow yourself to think, day by day and all day long.

It is altogether in your own hands. Nobody but yourself can keep you down. Nobody else can involve you in difficulty or limitation. Neither parents, nor wives, nor husbands, nor employers, nor neighbors; nor poverty, nor ignorance, nor any power whatever can keep you out of your own when once you have learned how to think.

The Science of Living is the Science of Thought.

DON'T BE A TRAGEDY QUEEN

WHEN things go seriously wrong there is a strong temptation to cast oneself for a tragic rôle, to feel deeply injured and even embittered. The result of this, however, is only to make it more difficult to get things right again. Indeed, it may be quite impossible to demonstrate at all so long as this attitude lasts.

Self pity, by making us feel sorry for ourselves, seems to provide an escape from responsibility, but it is a fatal drug nevertheless. It confuses the feelings, blinds the reason, and puts us at the mercy of outer conditions.

In the old-fashioned dramas a favorite rôle was the Tragedy Queen. It was traditional for her to stalk about the stage in heavy black with an intolerable air of injured innocence. She never made any attempt to put things right, and she invariably came to a sad end.

Don't be a tragedy queen—whether you are a man or a woman, for it is not a question of sex but of mental outlook. No matter what happens, refuse to take it tragically. Absolutely repudiate a crown of martyrdom. If you cannot laugh at yourself (which is the best medicine of all), at least try to handle the difficulty in an objective way, as though it concerned somebody else. To be tragic is to accept defeat. To refuse to be tragic is to affirm victory. Know that you can be victorious and insist upon victory. Realize: *God in me is stronger than anything I have to meet.*

FUNDAMENTAL TRUTH

THE principal revelation of the Jesus Christ Teaching is the Omnipresence and Availability of God, and the belief that because God not only transcends His universe but is everywhere immanent in it—that He indwells in it—it must in reality reflect His perfection. It is prayer which opens the door of the soul so that the Divine Power may work its will to harmony and peace.

This religion teaches that physical ailments are really maladies of the soul outpictured on the body, and that with the healing of the soul accomplished, the healing of the body must follow. The soul is vivified by drawing closer to God through prayer and meditation, and by changing one's outer conduct to bring it more completely in harmony with God's law.

It teaches the efficacy of Scientific Prayer to reshape one's whole life for health, harmony, and spiritual development. By Scientific Prayer we mean the Practice of the Presence of God.

61

CAFETERIA

DON'T wait for something to turn up. Don't be content to let things drift along, hoping for the best. It is not spiritual to "put up" with inharmonious conditions. If the conditions of your life are not to your liking, you must get to work on your own consciousness and, by raising that above the outer picture, cause those conditions to become something nearer to your heart's desire; and you must keep on doing this until you find your True Place.

I had an amusing experience when I first came to America. Passing an attractive looking restaurant, I went inside, and, selecting a table, sat down and waited. Strangely, as it seemed to me then, nothing happened. I sat there and continued to wait—indefinitely as it seemed. I could not understand the reason for this neglect. All around me, people were enjoying their food, and only I was left out in the cold.

After a while the truth of the situation slowly dawned on me—it was a cafeteria. (This system had not yet made its appearance in England in those days.)

I then quickly realized that while there was plenty of food of every kind to be obtained, one had to go forward and claim it for himself, or go without.

The universe is run exactly on the lines of a cafeteria. Unless you claim—mentally —what you want, you may sit and wait forever. Of course, you should not claim in detail—that is outlining—but you must positively claim health, harmony, and True Place, if you really want those things.

PROBLEMS AND
OPPORTUNITIES

THANKSGIVING DAY, 1936, finds us at a point in world history where, upon the threshold of the New Age, we are confronted by major problems of every kind. I think I cannot do better than quote here what I wrote three years ago in the pamphlet, *The Historical Destiny of the United States*:

"Now, does all this mean that I think that the future history of the United States is going to be a simple and easy path of uninterrupted development? No, I do not suppose anything of the kind. The fact is, that a quiet and uneventful life is rather the mark of age and decrepitude than of youth and vigor. It is the destiny of youth to have great problems and great difficulties to tackle and to solve, and it is the glory of youth to have the vision and the energy to do both without fear. When the life of a man or of a nation becomes gentle and

64

uneventful, it means that its work is done;
but the work of this nation is only beginning,
and I expect, therefore, that in the years
ahead of us there will be great problems
and difficulties and even dangers to be met
and overcome. But I know that as long as
the American people are true to themselves,
and to the American Dream; as long, that
is to say, as they remain united in essentials,
so long will they continue to remain unde-
feated; and so long will they fulfil their
destiny of service to the world. Difficulties
and problems are good things in themselves
because every difficulty overcome is proof
of a further advance in consciousness."

THE SUPREME RIGHT

IN the long run, no one can retain what does not belong to him by right of consciousness, nor be deprived of that which is truly his by the same supreme title.

Therefore, you will do well not to lay up to yourself treasures upon earth, but rather to lay up treasure in heaven; that is, the understanding of Spiritual Law. If you are looking to outer, passing, mutable things for either happiness or security, you are not putting God first. If you are putting God first in your life, you will not find yourself laboring under undue anxiety about anything, for *where your treasure is, there will your heart be also.*

From *The Sermon on the Mount*

YOUR GOOD IS ETERNAL

IS IT not a beautiful and encouraging thought that all the prayers you have ever said in your life, and all the good deeds and kind words for which you have ever been responsible are still with you, and that nothing can ever take them away? Indeed, our prayers and our words and acts of kindness to others are the only things that we ever do keep, for all the rest must disappear. Errors of thought, word, and deed are worked out and satisfied under the Law, but the good goes on forever, unchanged and undimmed by time.

From *The Sermon on the Mount*

THE GREAT HIPPODROME MEETING

THE success of the meeting at the Hippodrome on March 14 exceeded all expectations. Long before 10 o'clock, a crowd of people filled the sidewalk for the whole block and down 44th Street, and by the time the service started over six thousand people were crammed into the huge auditorium. People sat on the steps and around the gangways, and the lobbies were also filled, these having been provided with loud speakers.

It was undoubtedly the greatest meeting that has ever been held in the Truth movement, and it is a wonderful proof of the eager desire that people have today for a demonstrable religion which is purely spiritual.

One of the striking features of the service was the wonderful character of the meditation. The vast audience maintained perfect silence for four minutes without any sense of strain or effort, contemplating the thought: *The Christ of God is reborn in me today with great power.*

In the sermon it was stressed that the second coming of the Christ is the coming of this Truth to the general public in this age as never before. Hitherto, throughout the ages, individuals and small groups have understood the All-ness and Availability of God, but now for the first time the mass of mankind is to receive it. This is the heralding of a new age of individual demonstration. In consequence of this revolutionary change in thought in the people's minds, all sorts of natural, political, and social upheavals will be seen for a few years, but as the new understanding begins to work out, an era of great peace, harmony, and unprecedented progress will dawn for humanity.

SHOW ME THY FACE!

SHOW me Thy face—one transient gleam
  Of loveliness divine,
And I shall never think or dream
  Of other love than Thine;
All other light will darken quite,
  All lower glories wane,
The beautiful of earth will scarce
  Seem beautiful again.

Show me Thy face—I shall forget
  The weary days of yore;
The fretting thoughts of vain regret
  Shall hurt my soul no more;
All doubts and fears for future years
  In quiet trust subside,
And naught but blest content and calm
  Within my breast reside.

SPARKS OF TRUTH

Show me Thy face—the heaviest cross
　　Will then seem light to bear;
There will be gain in every loss
　　And peace with every care.
With such light feet the years will fleet,
　　Life seem as brief as blest;
Till I have laid my burden down
　　And entered into rest.

(Psalm 102: 1, 2)

* This poem is a wonderful treatment. The author is unknown.